Shirt Designer Book

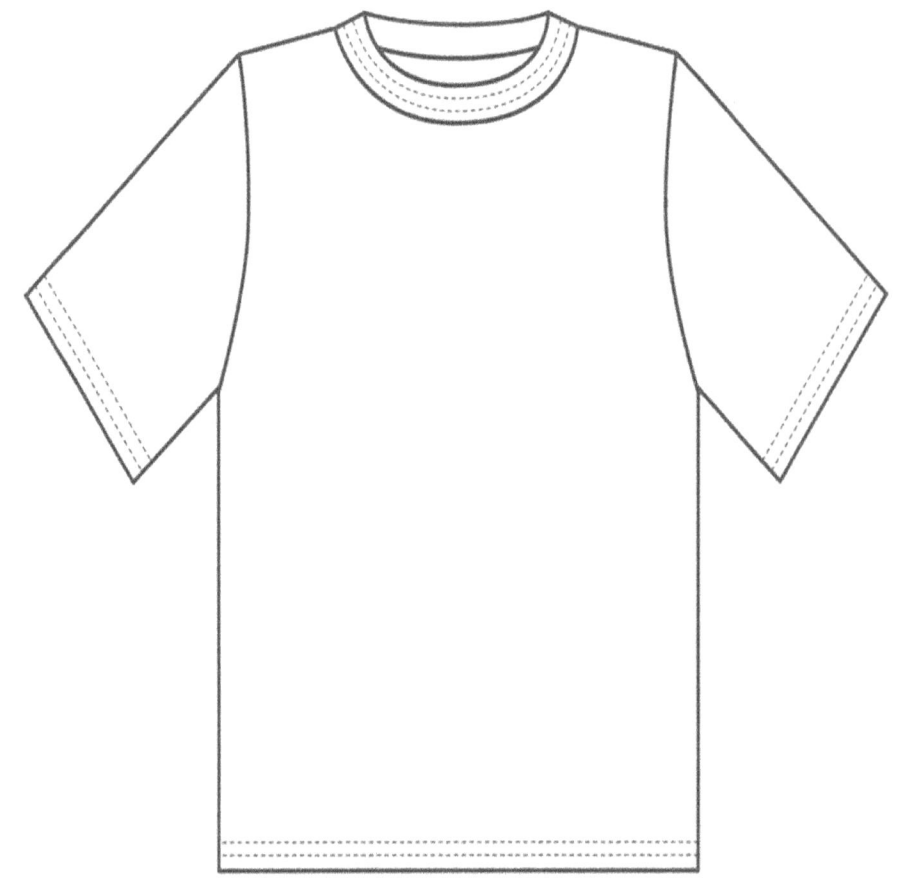

FRONT

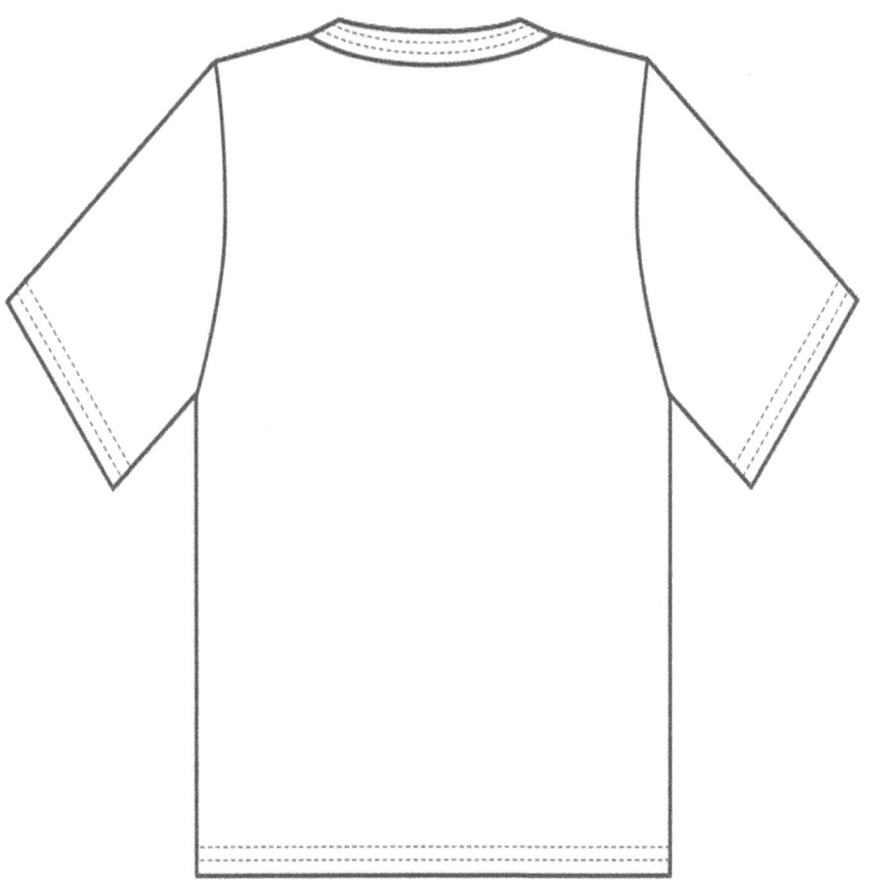

BACK

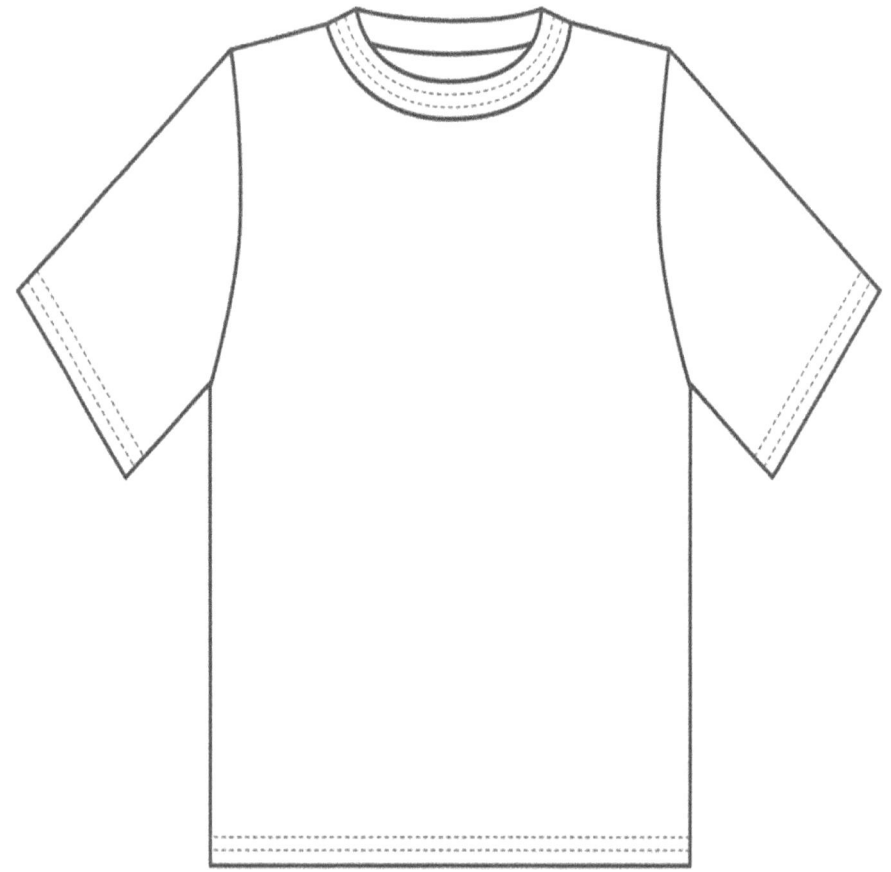

FRONT

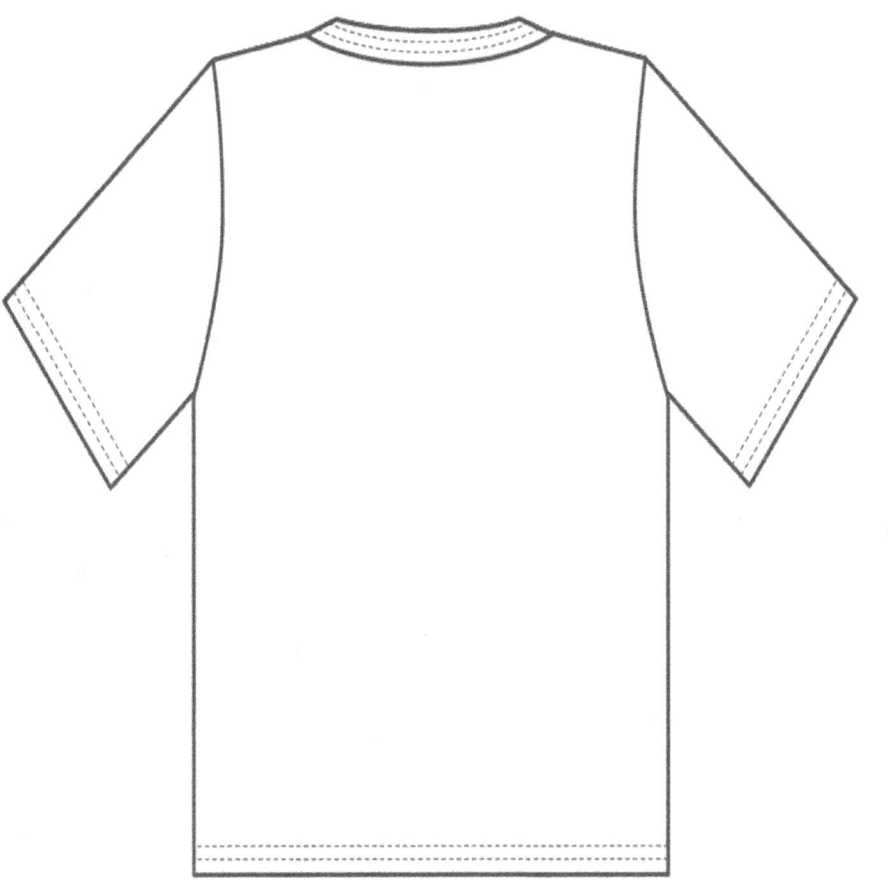

BACK

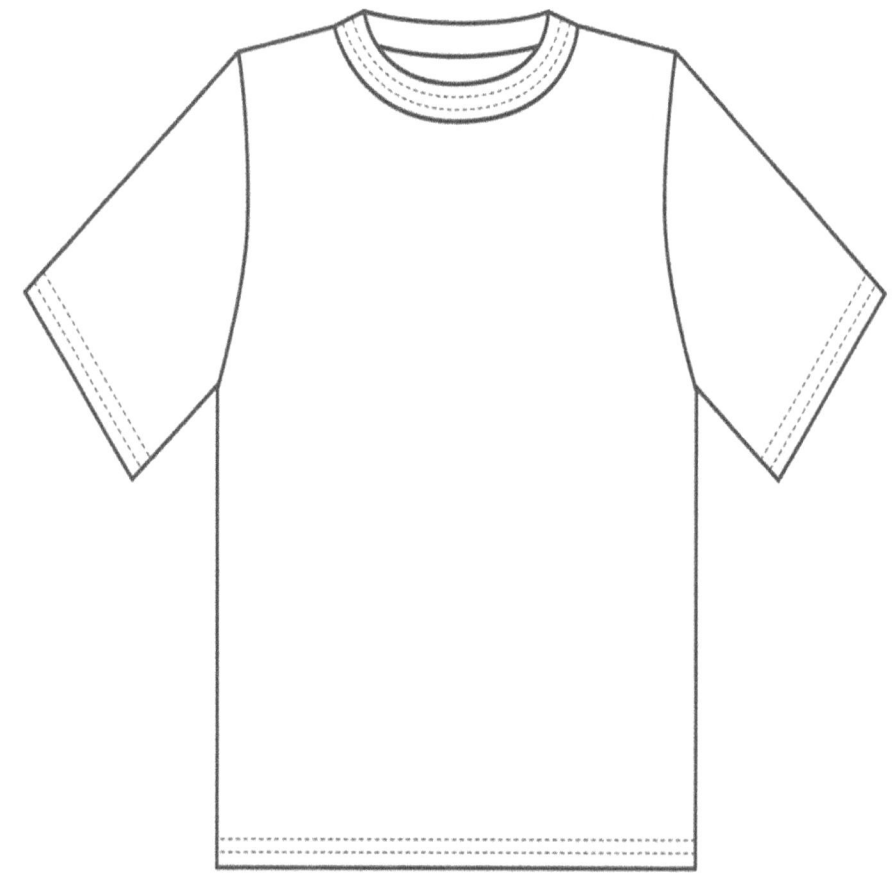

FRONT

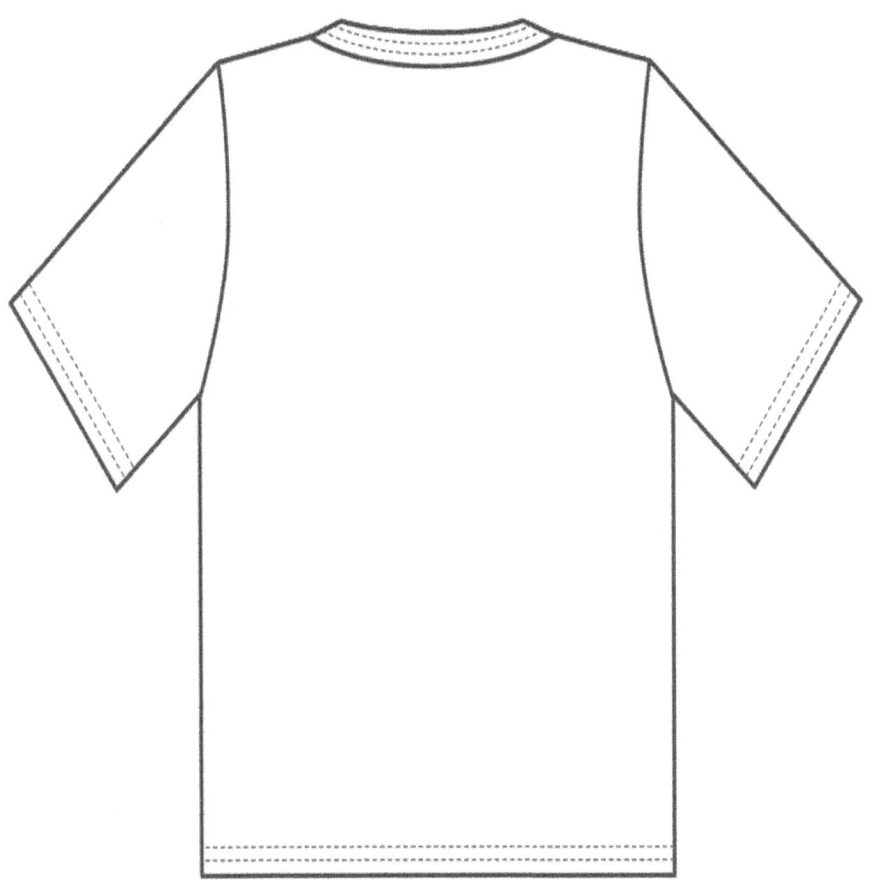

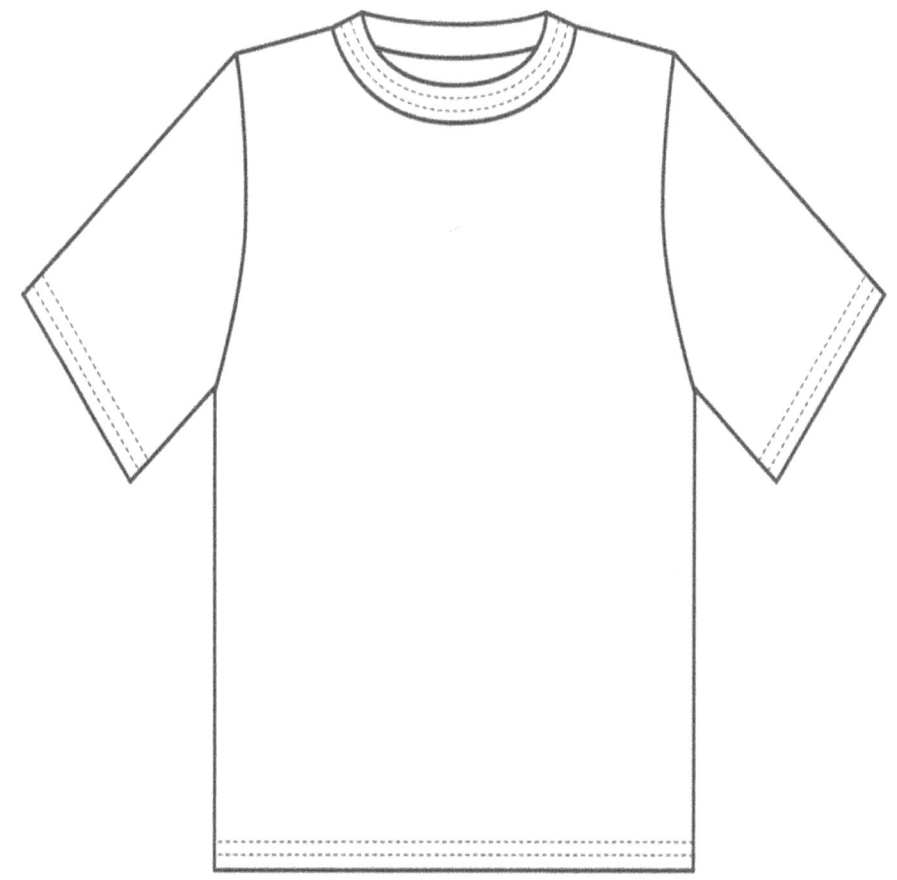

FRONT

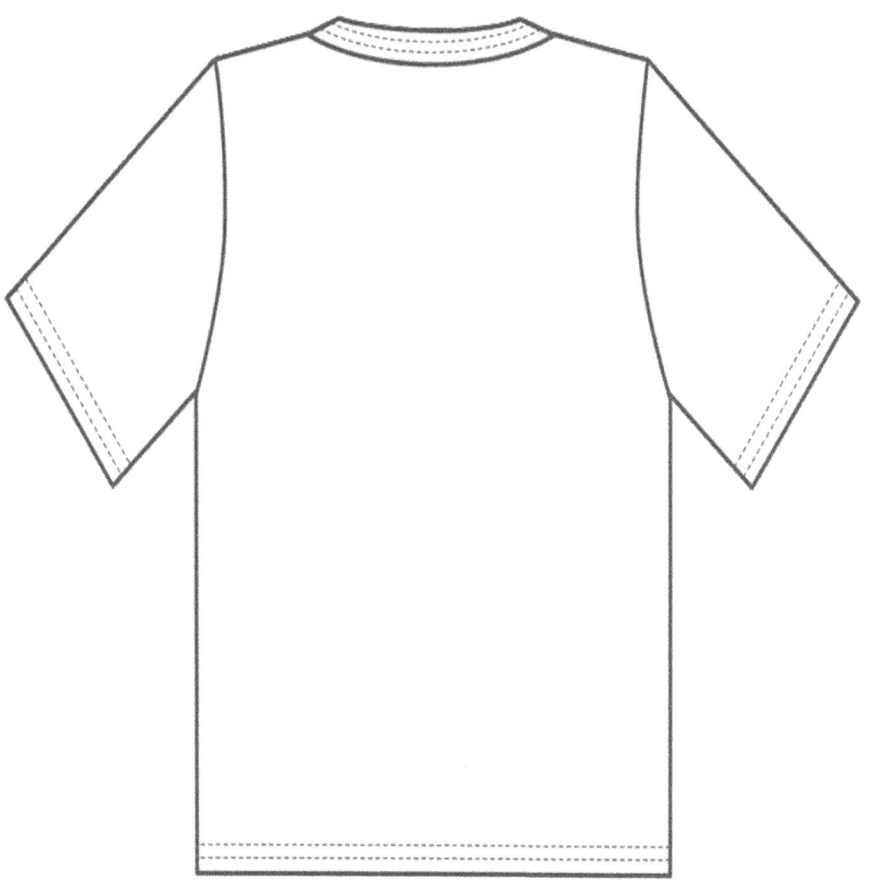

BACK

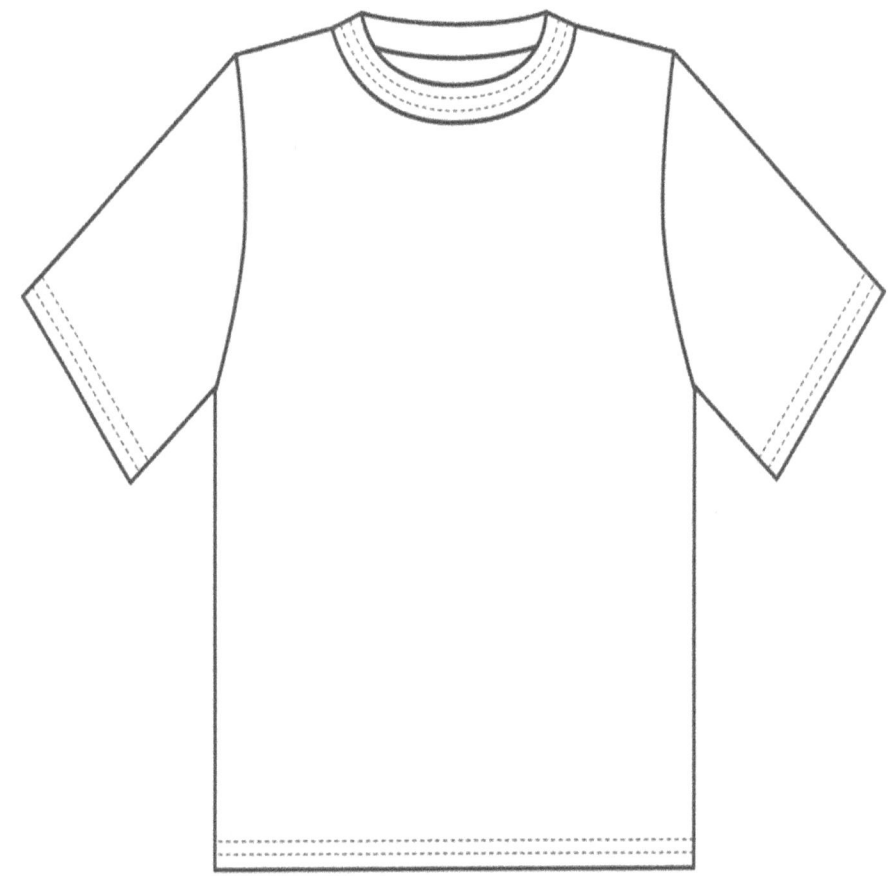

FRONT

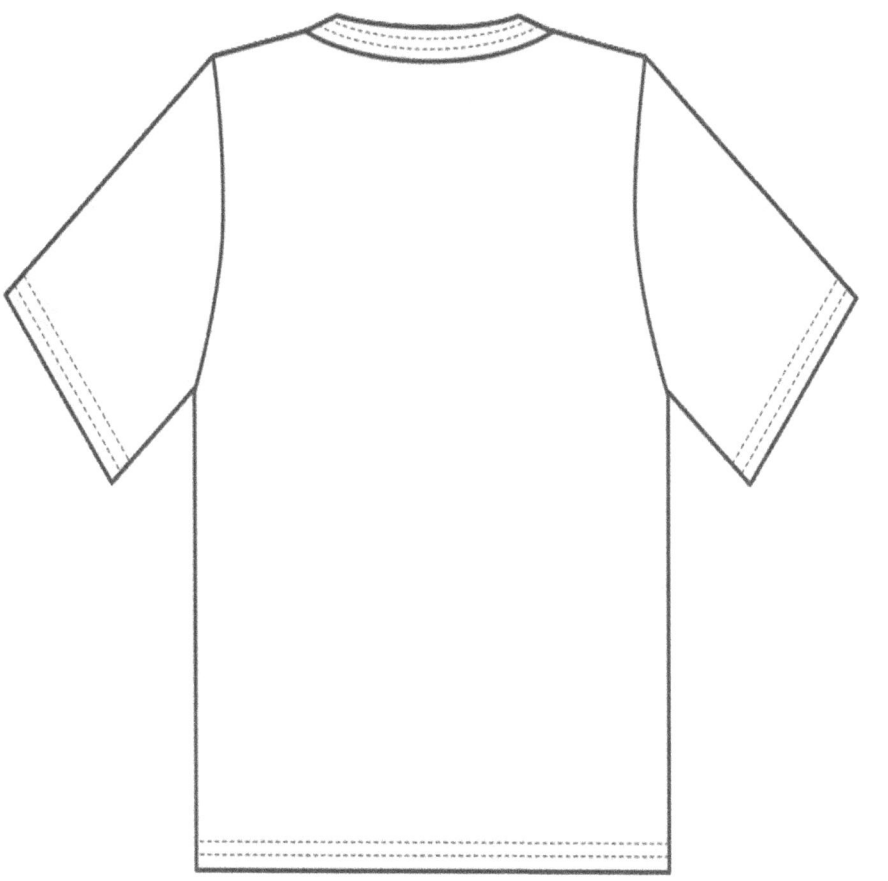

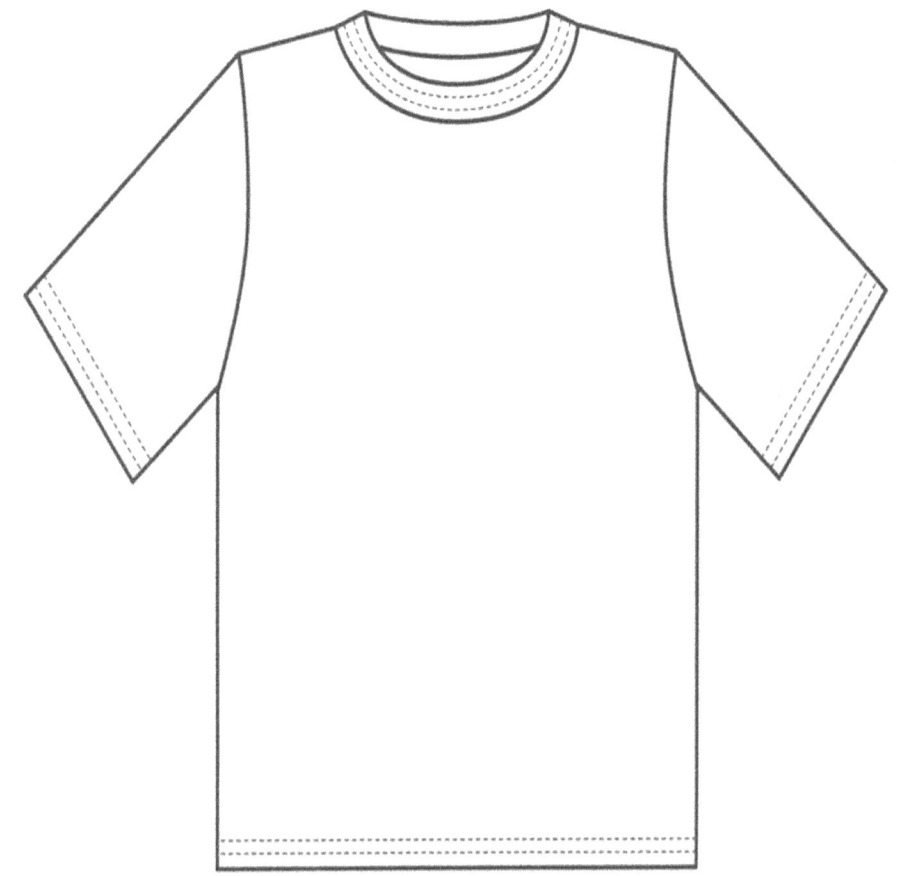

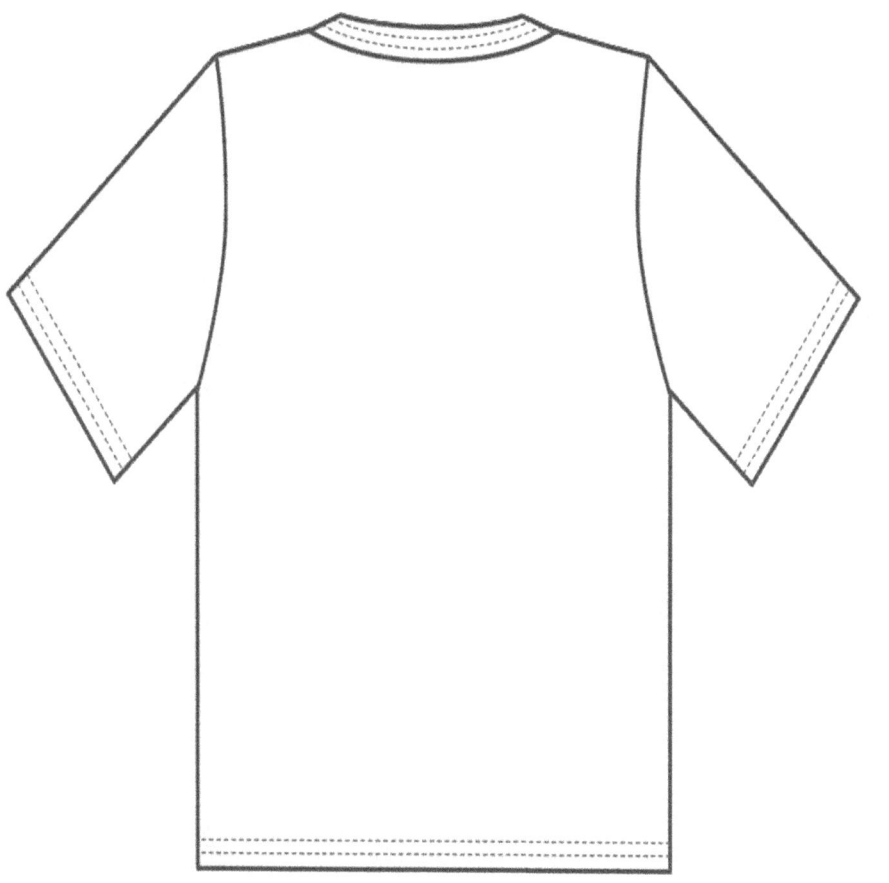

BACK

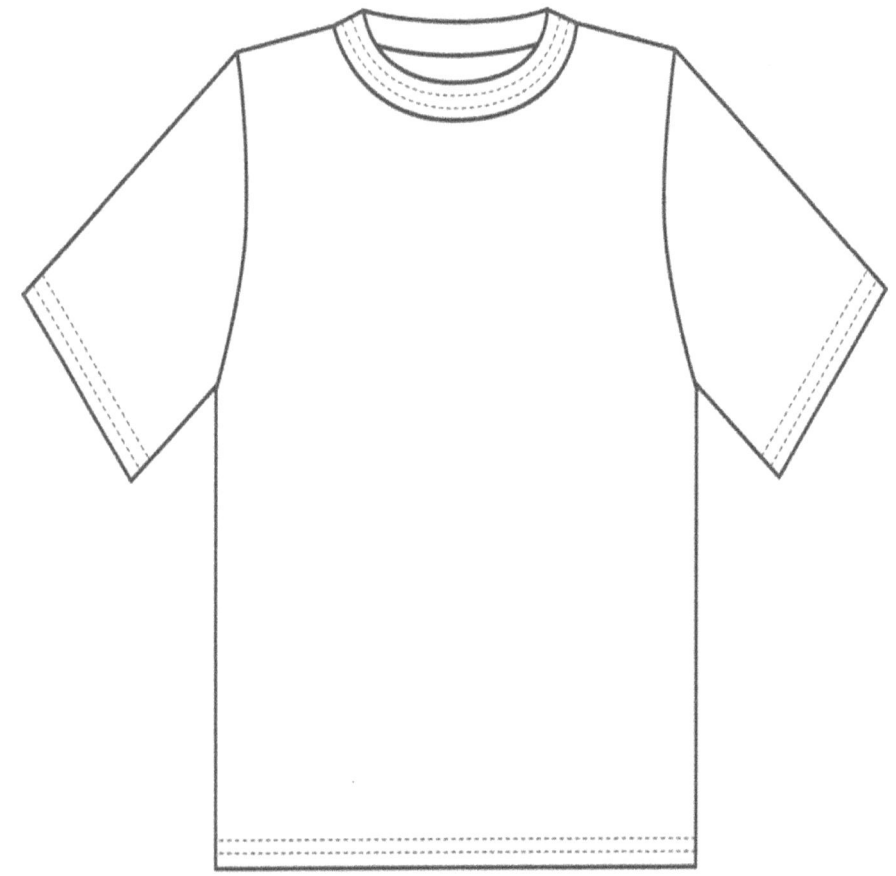

FRONT

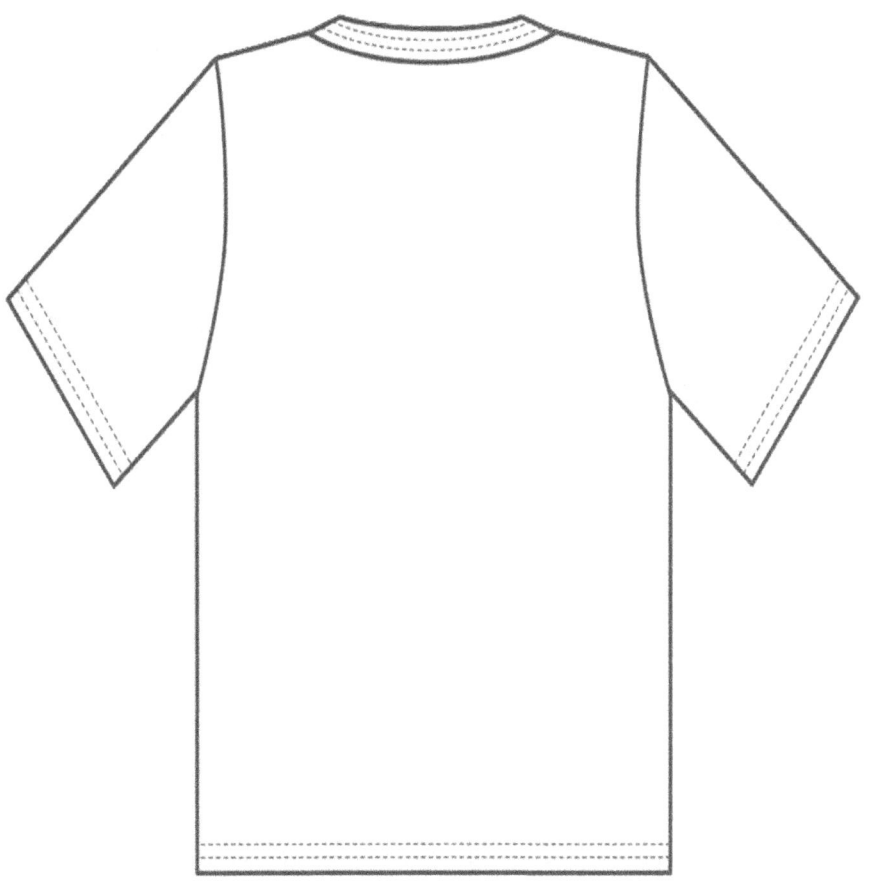

BACK

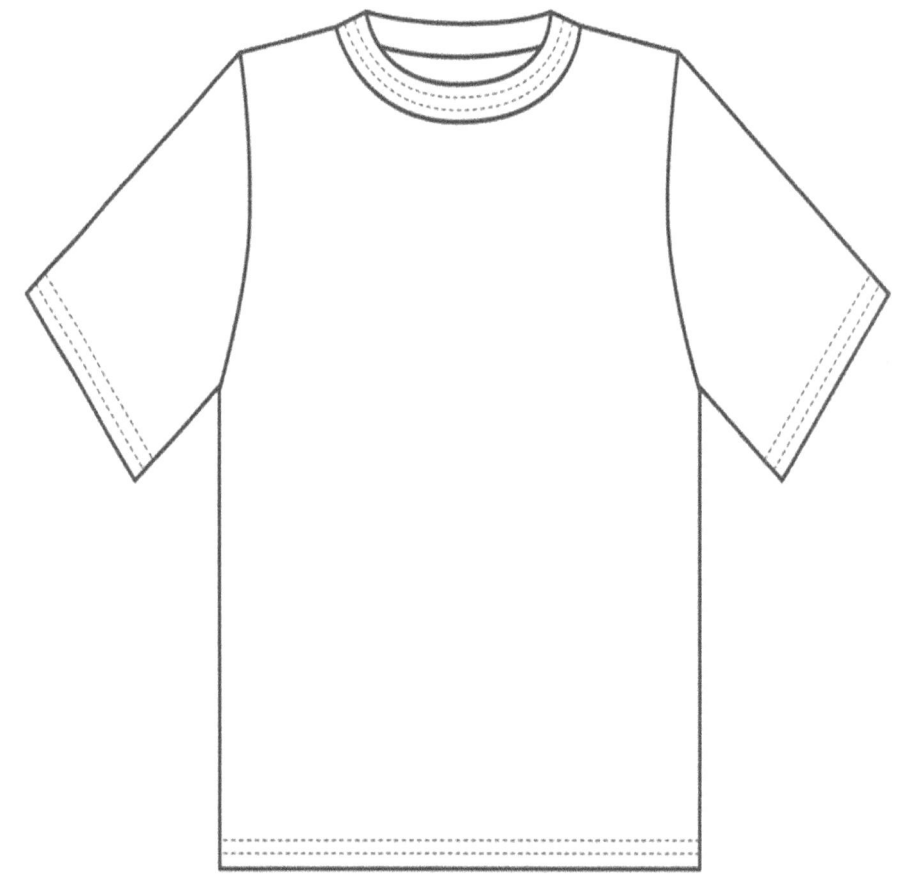

FRONT

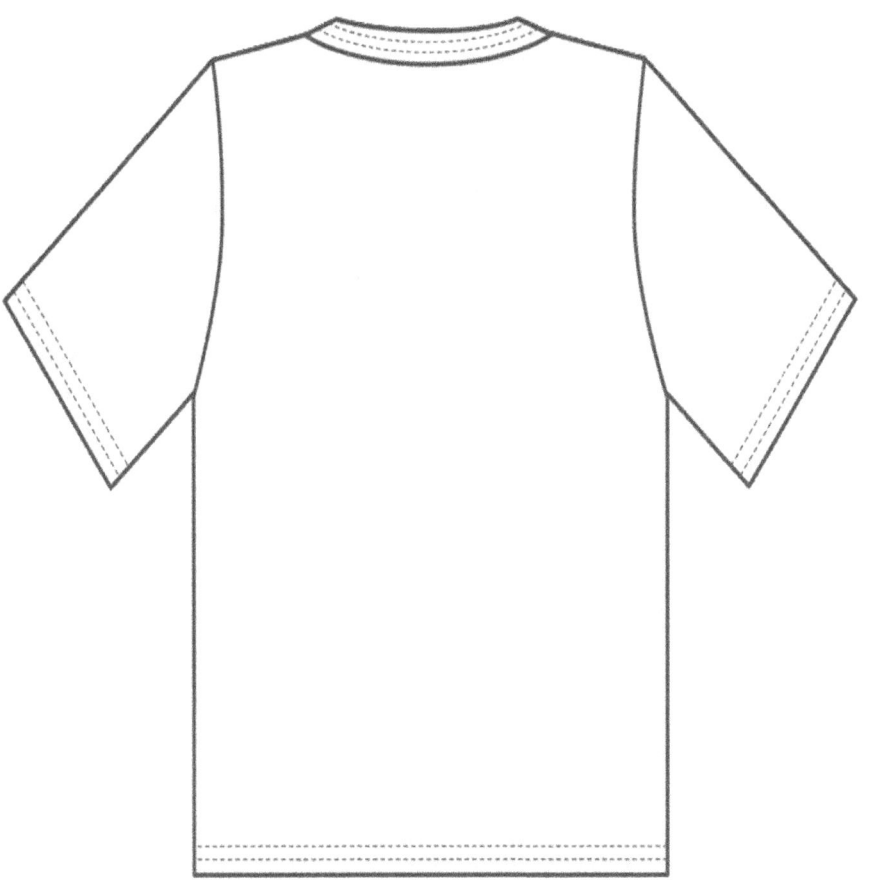

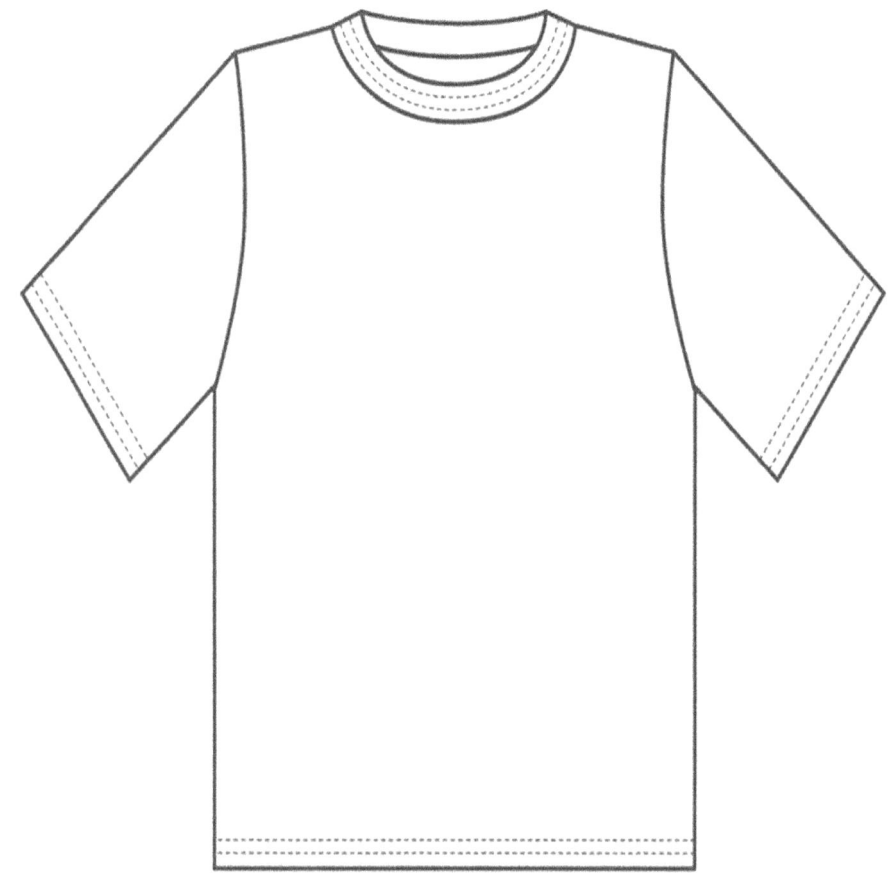

FRONT

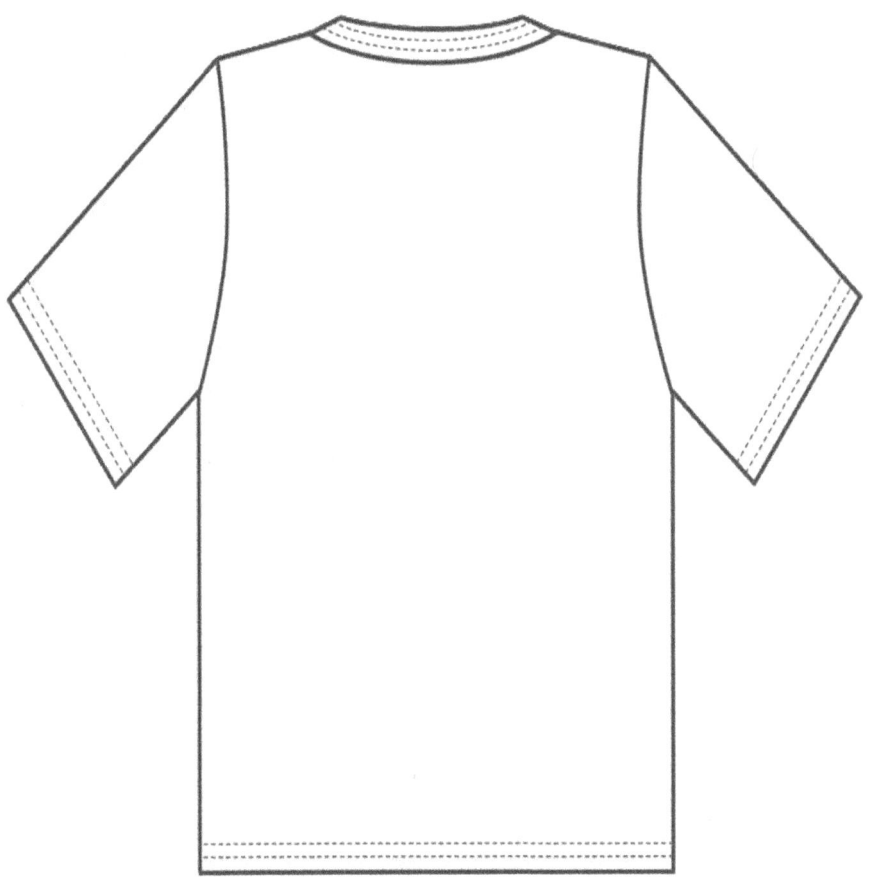

BACK

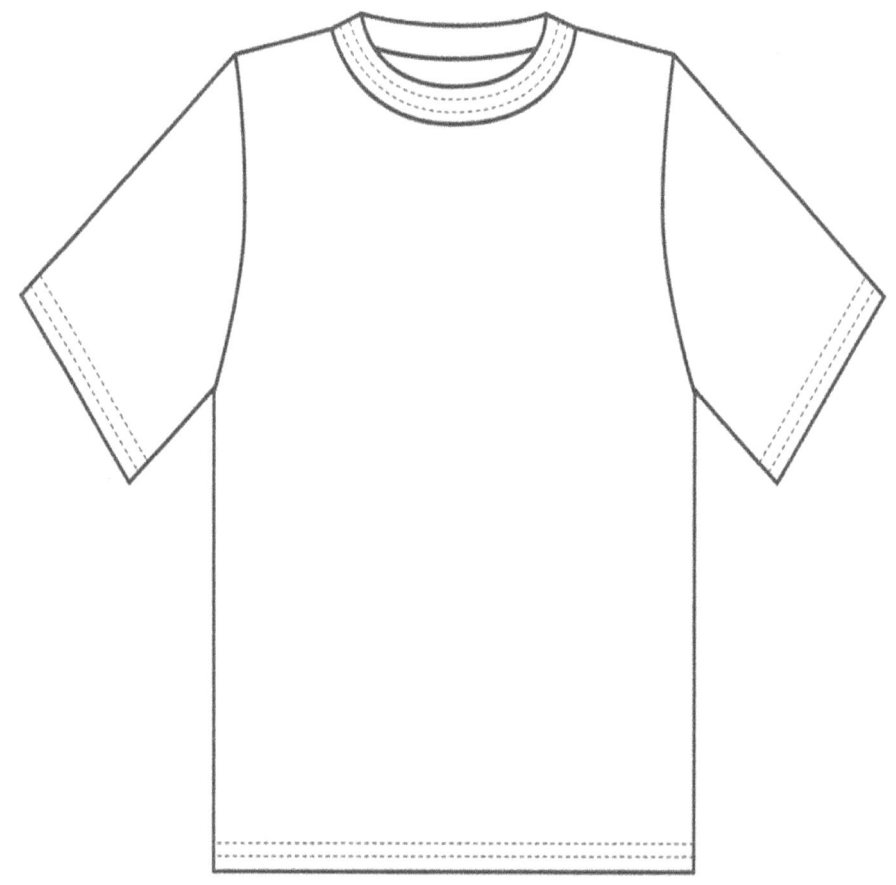

FRONT

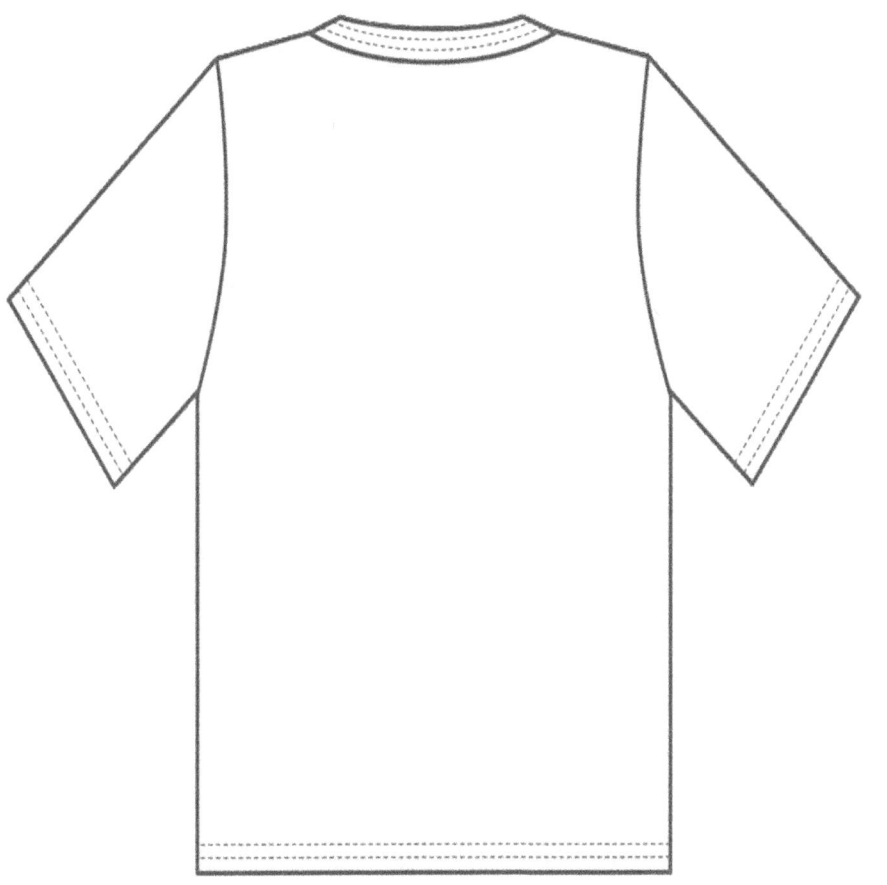

BACK

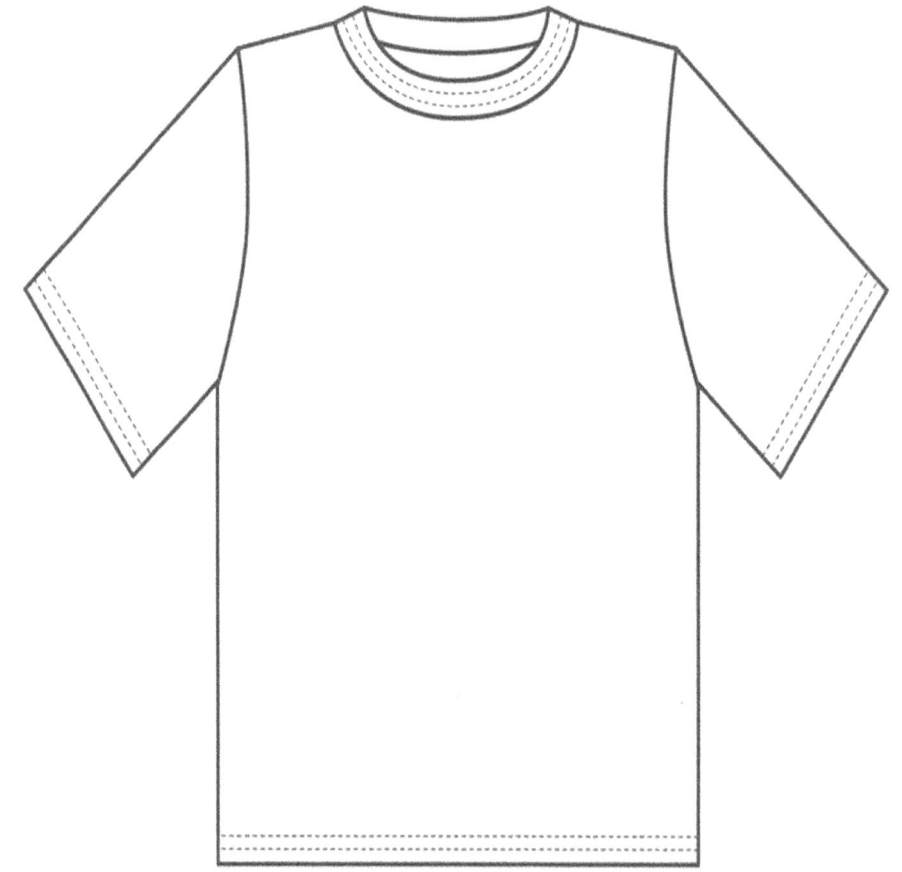

FRONT

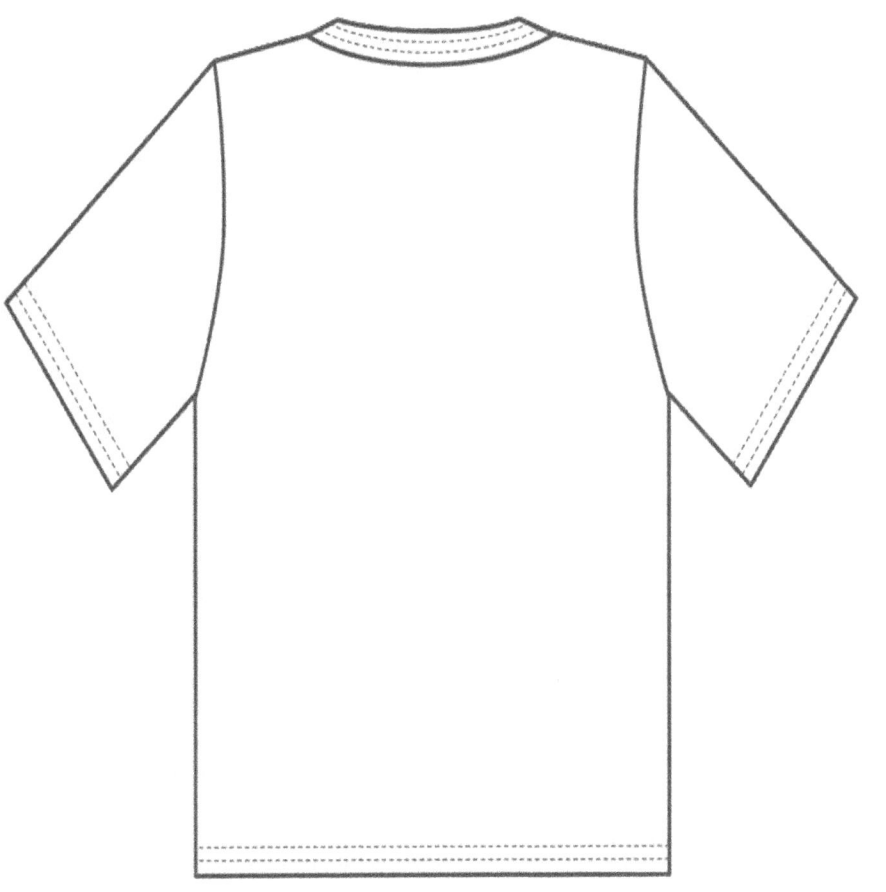

BACK

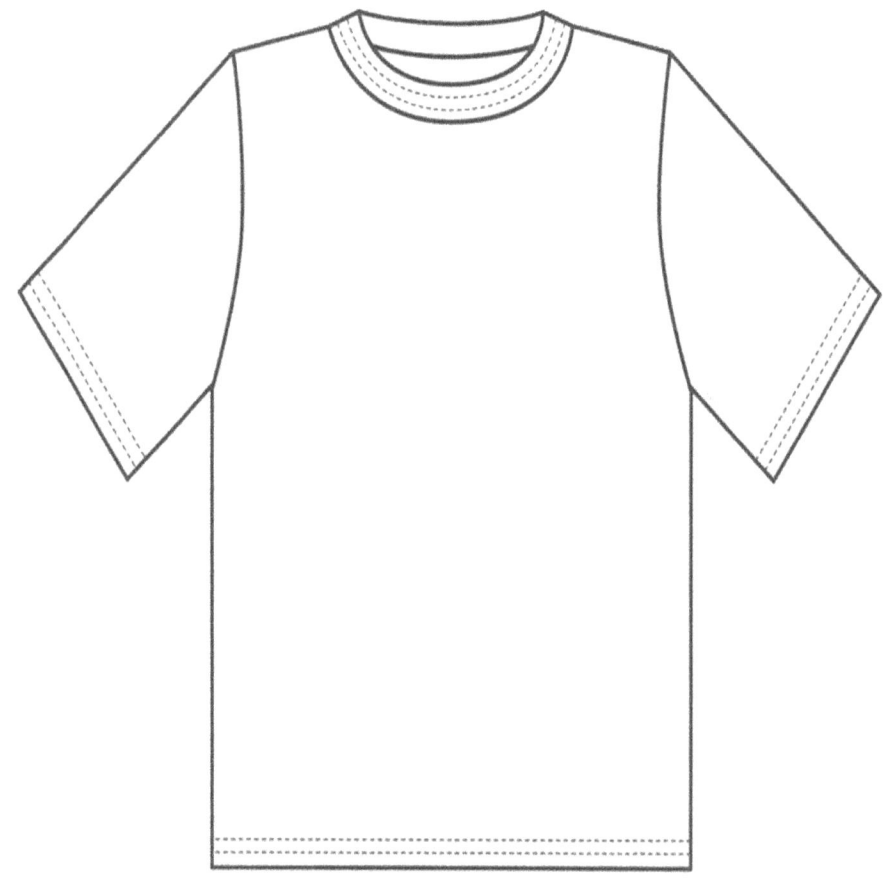

FRONT

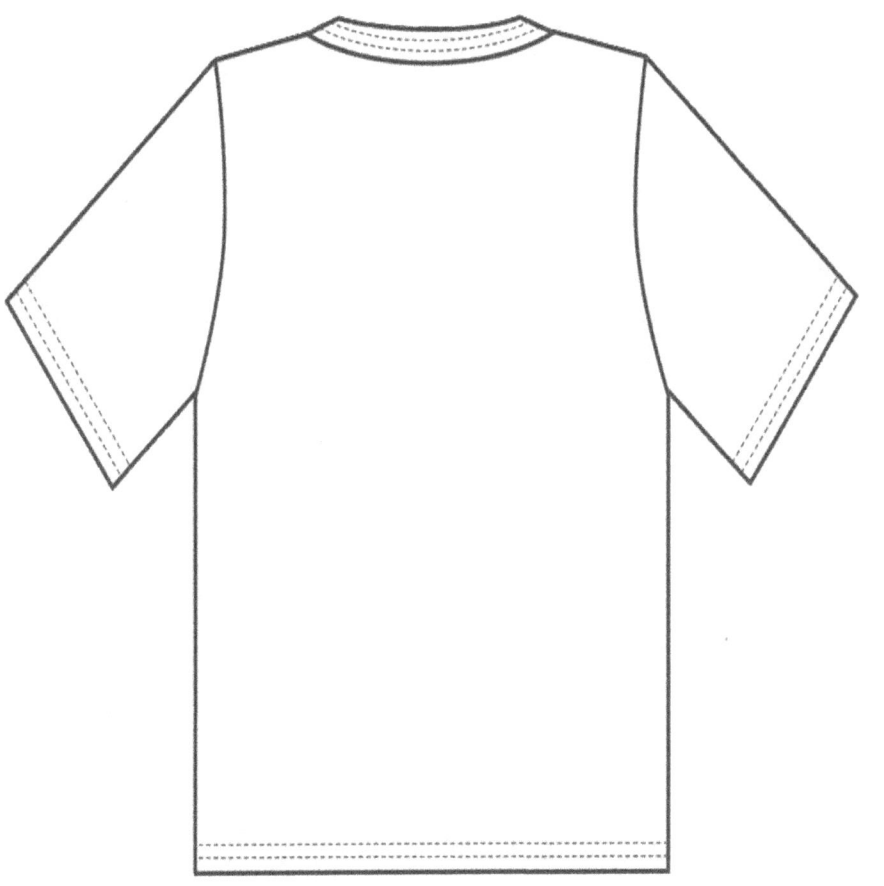

BACK

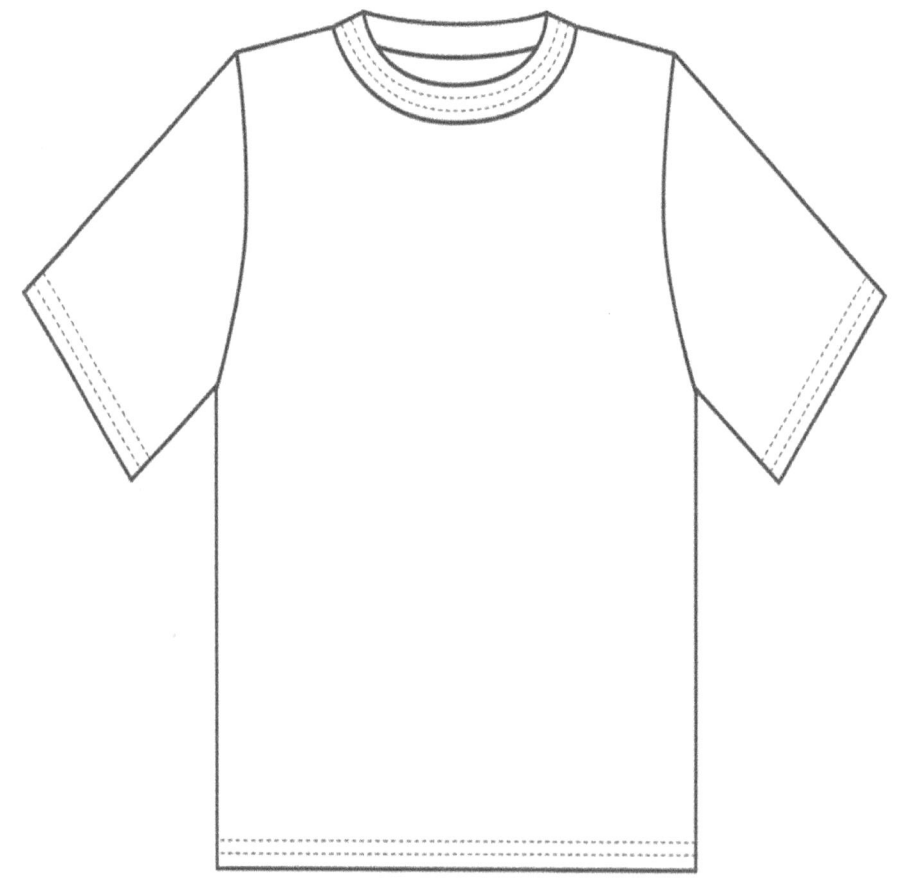

FRONT

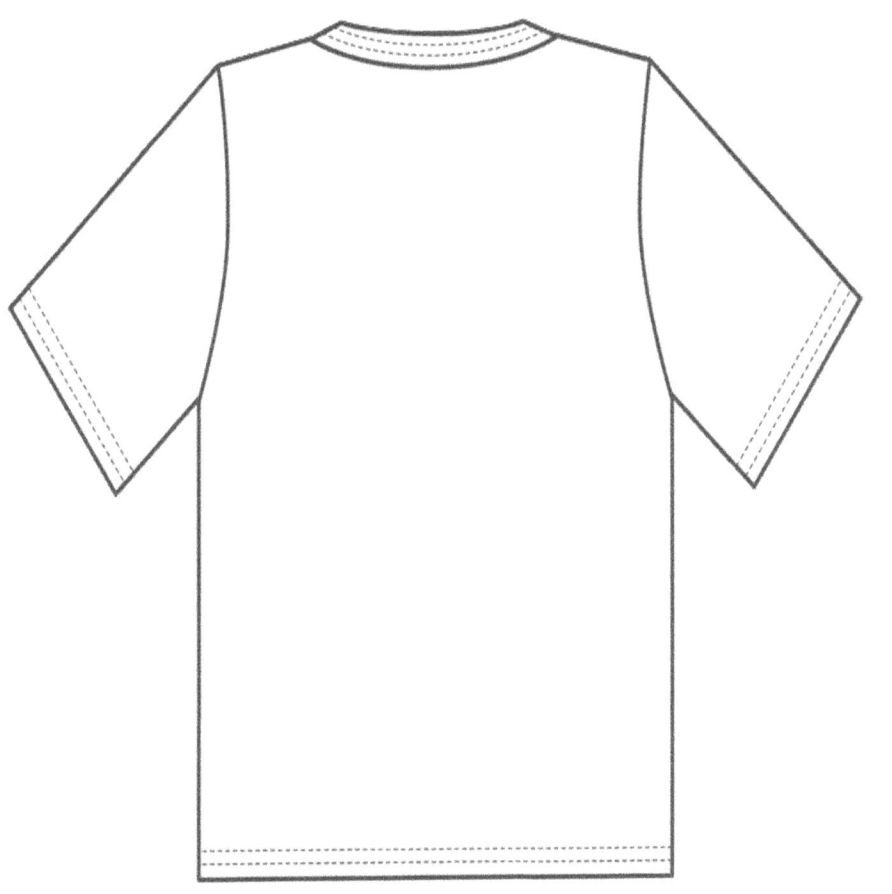

BACK

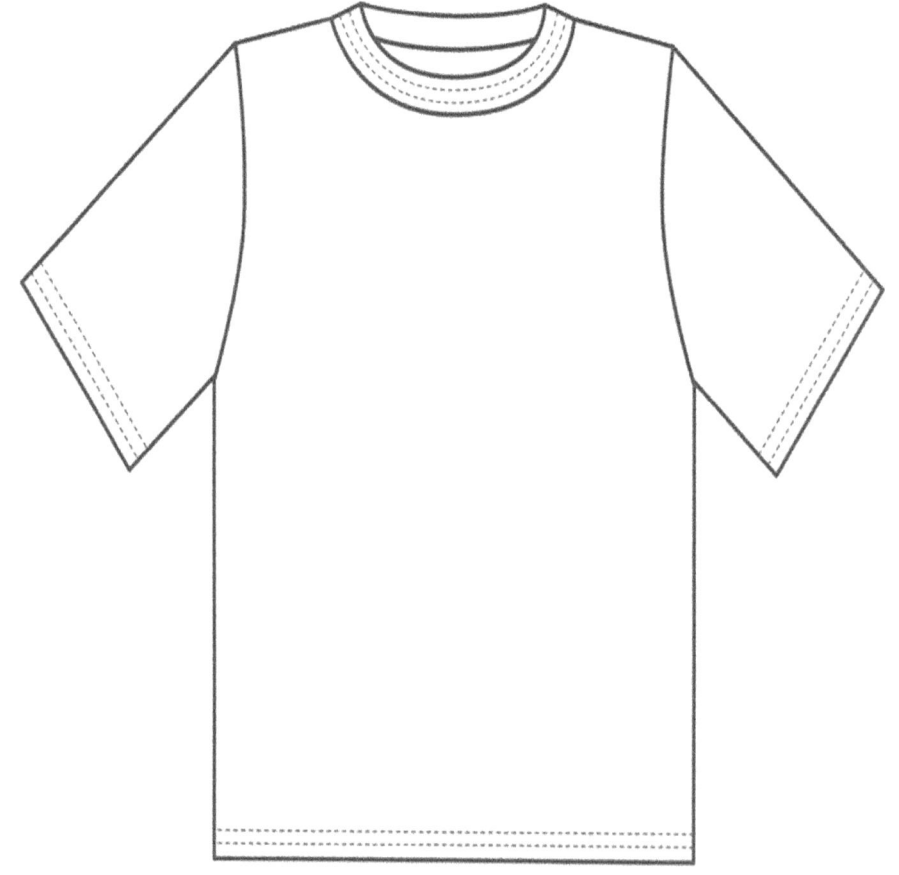

FRONT

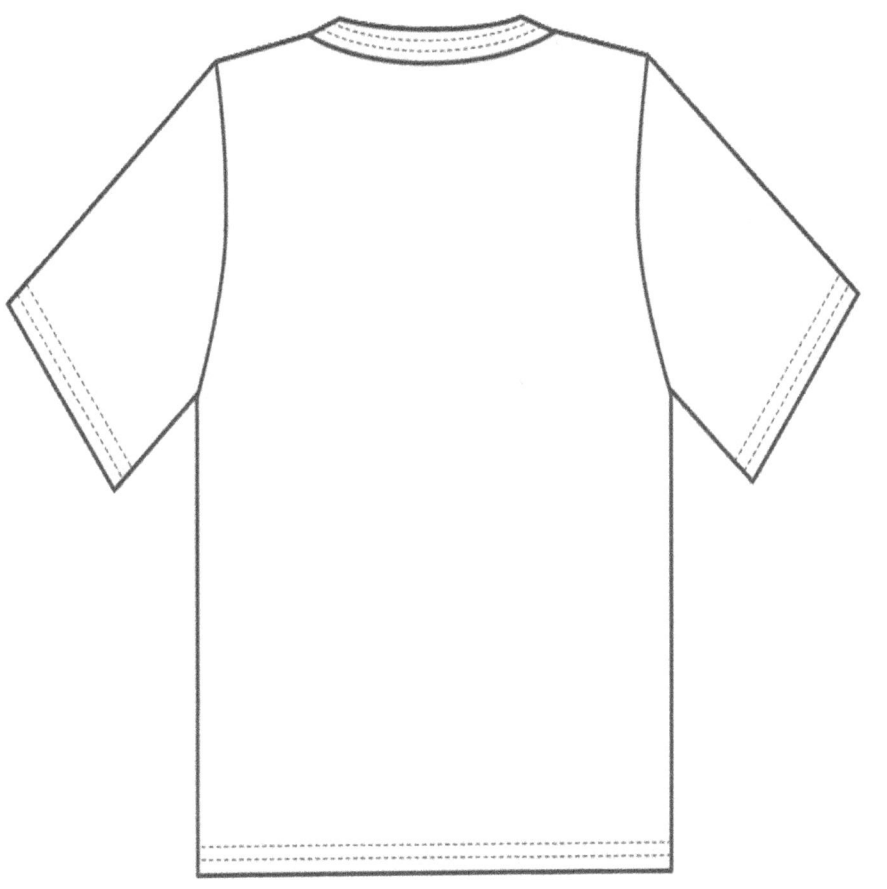

BACK

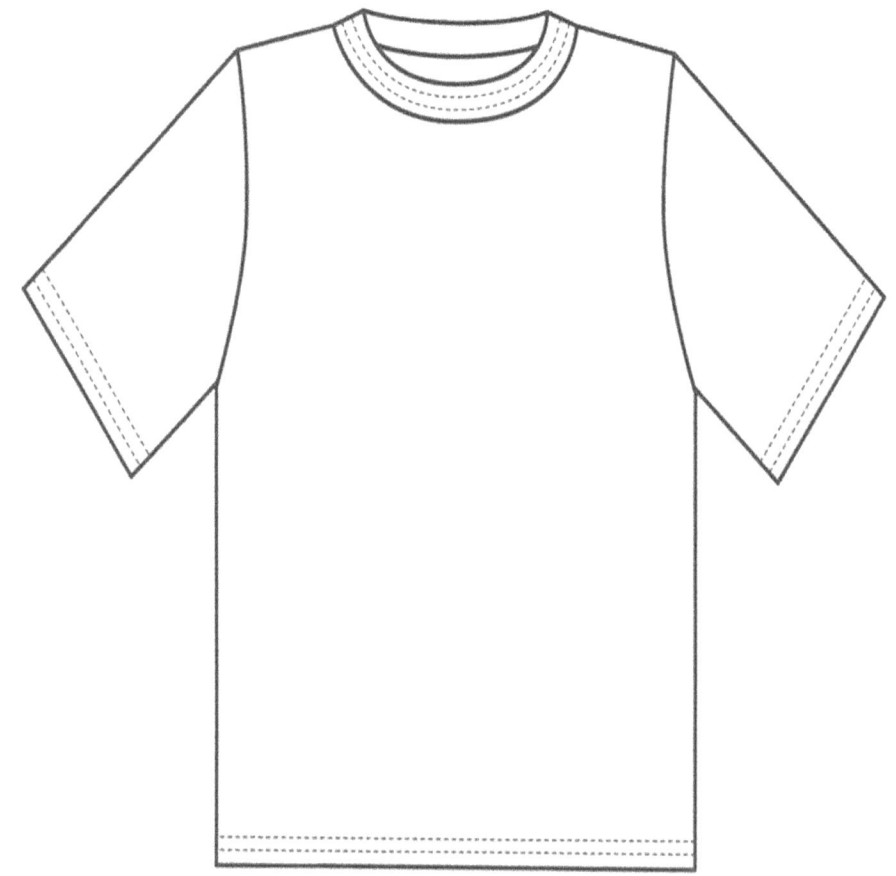

FRONT

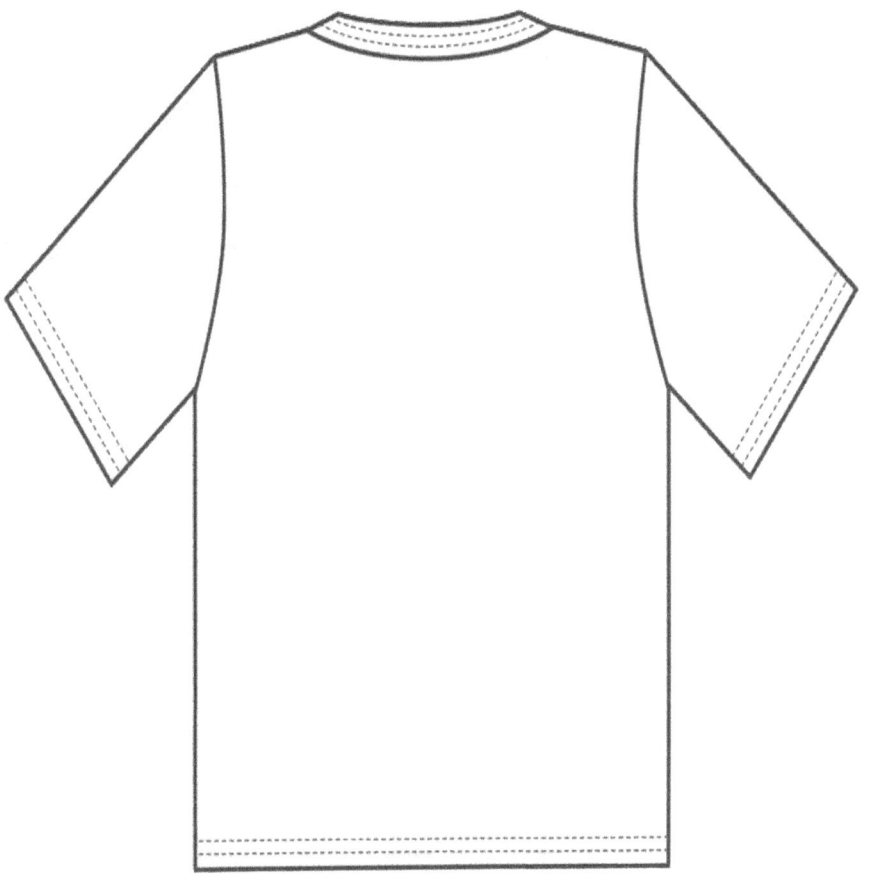

BACK

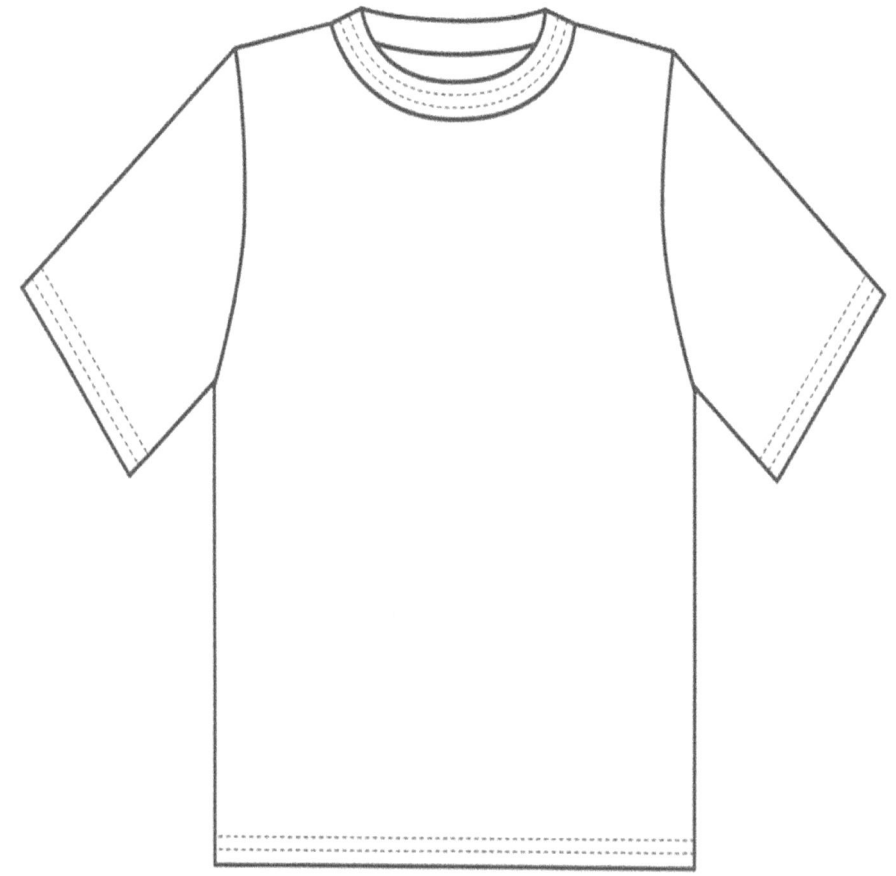

FRONT

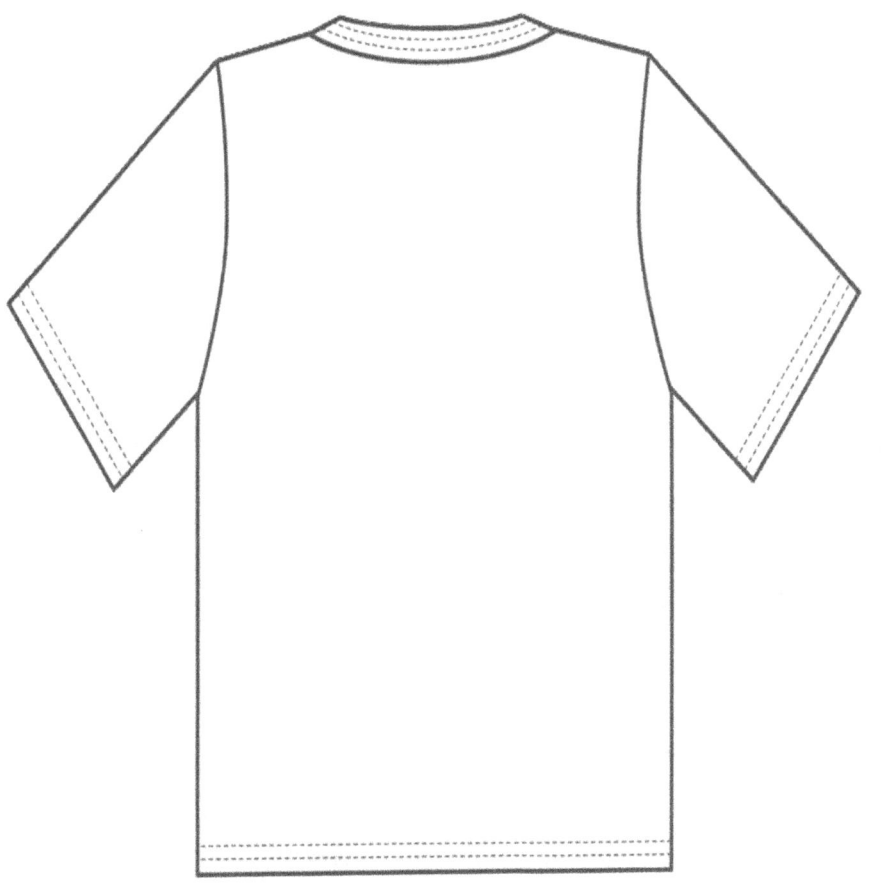

BACK

www.ingramcontent.com/pod-product-compliance
Lightning Source LLC
Chambersburg PA
CBHW030105230526
45471CB00003B/1264